GORILLAS

by Ruth Mattison

Pioneer Valley Educational Press, Inc.

TABLE OF CONTENTS

GENTLE GIANTS

Gorillas are the largest **primates**.

Sometimes in movies, gorillas
are made to appear to be dangerous
and **violent**, but gorillas
are mostly peaceful, gentle, and shy.

FAMILY LIFE

Male gorillas are much larger than females and weigh almost twice as much. Adult male gorillas are called silverbacks because they have a patch of silver hair on their backs.

Silverbacks are the leaders of a group called a troop. Each silverback leads a troop of 5 to 30 gorillas that live together.

The leader decides where the troop
will travel for food each day,
when they will stop to eat or rest,
and where they will spend the night.

Sometimes, a younger male from a different troop challenges the troop leader.
To scare off this intruder, the troop leader beats his chest, screams, bares his teeth, and then charges forward. He may even break off tree branches and shake them at the intruder until the intruder leaves.

HABITAT AND FOOD

Gorillas live in Africa. Some live in the mountains. Others live in the lowlands in forests, swamps, and marshes.

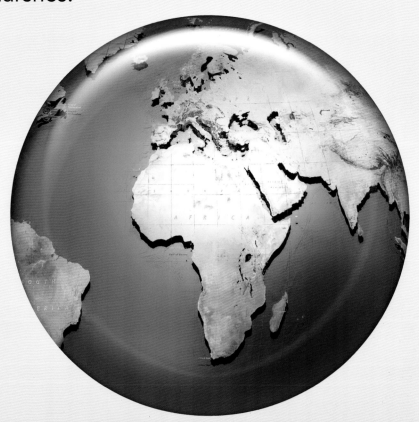

Every morning, the silverback leads
his troop to a new place where there is
plenty of food for all of them to eat.

After eating all morning, the adult gorillas
gather leaves, twigs, and branches
to make a nest for resting.
After resting, the gorillas eat again
until bedtime. Then they make another nest.
Gorillas rarely use the same nest twice.

Gorillas are mostly vegetarians.
They eat fruit, leaves, and plant shoots,
but sometimes they eat small insects.

Gorillas have long teeth and can crush
hard plants like bamboo.

BABY GORILLAS

Female gorillas begin looking for a mate when they are about 8 years old. They leave the safety of their own troop and begin to search for another troop or a single silverback to live with.

A newborn gorilla can be much smaller than a human baby. They weigh only about 3 to 4 pounds when they are born. Baby gorillas drink their mothers' milk for the first 2½ years of life.

When baby gorillas are **weaned**, they begin
to build their own sleeping nests each day.
Young gorillas stay with their mothers
for 3 to 4 years.

Newborns grow quickly.
At 5 to 6 months old, they learn to walk,
and by 18 months of age, they can
follow their mothers on foot
for short distances. Still, the safest place
for youngsters is on their mothers' backs
as they travel through the **dense**
vegetation of their forest home.

Young gorillas wrestle and play games with each other. They learn some behaviors by **imitating** adult gorillas.

Even though gorillas do not have natural enemies, they are endangered. Some people hunt gorillas for food. Other people hunt gorillas just for fun.

Gorillas have lost large amounts of their forest **habitat**. Logging companies have cut down and removed trees from the forests where the gorillas live. In some places where gorillas live, people have cut down the forest trees to use the wood for fuel or to make way for farmland.

There are people trying to help gorillas survive.
There are scientists, park rangers,
and many other people who are working hard
to protect the gorillas and the forests
where they live in Africa.
There are new laws that limit the hunting
of gorillas and prevent the destruction
of the gorillas' habitat.

GLOSSARY

dense: thick

habitat: the natural place in which an animal lives

imitating: copying

primates: members of the biological order Primates

violent: uncontrolled, strong, rough force

weaned: when a baby animal stops drinking the mother's milk

INDEX